Poems That Urge The Soul

VOLUME 1

Alvin Othto Stewart

STEW-PENDOUS, INC.

Copyright © 2006
by Stew-Pendous, Inc.
Copyright secured U.S.A.
All rights reserved.
ISBN 10: 0-9785452-0-6
ISBN 13: 978-0-9785452-0-8

LCCN: Available upon request

Printed in the U.S.A.
Gorham Printing, Rochester, Washington

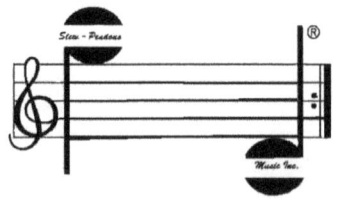

POEMS
THAT URGE
THE SOUL

VOLUME 1

Winners Are Really Losers
Who Never Give Up

A wrong turn in life can side track a dream
But things are never ever as bad as they may seem.
If you just believe you've got the strength inside
To weather any storm once you really try.
Only sheer determination
Can lift you from this rut
Remember, winners are really losers
Who never give up.

So make the right choice and turn your life around
Lift your soul from Hell and put your feet on solid ground.
The values of existing, a mind must rearrange
Or you could spend a lifetime feeling things will never change.
When you feel there's no tomorrow
And you're about to self-destruct
Remember, winners are really losers
Who never give up.

So when the cards are not in your favor
And you're so down on your luck
Remember, winners are really losers
Who never give up

A Closet Full Of Fashion Moths

To those pesty wardrobe ruiners

A closet full of fashion moths
Weigh their convictions.
Were they meritorious,
With all their afflictions?

"We mode this hat of tattered felt
Until it was insecure.
And burrowed deep when rain would pelt
That worn trench coat's armature.

How often did we penetrate
These suits that couldn't resist.
And drill our holes in every dress
With excavated bliss.

Piercing all purpose jeans,
And perforating sneakers.
Where we're forced to share attire
With other crawly creatures."

Finally, inside out, and outside in
One garment to another
They chose the clothes that set the trend,
And bore praise to each other.

A Poet's Plight

To writer's cramps

I write because I have no choice
Words get in the way
You say I'm blessed, I have a voice
And so many ways to say
How stimulating or aggravating
A day in life can be
While I must constantly wrestle with
A way for you to see

Hours of thoughtless energy
Waste while patient verse
Borders on insanity
When a subject's over rehearsed

Pity you have no time to thaw
This ever present madness
Too busy being entertained
By the gladness or the sadness

I envy your born luxury
Still I can't deny
Without this poet's agony
I could not comply.

"Amigo, You Got Cookies"

To my little friends at play.

They're a lovely little ruckus bunch
Who stampede
For rambunctious needs
Up and down the hallway outside my door.
They laugh and play and sometimes fight for
Recognition,
Which elevates my condition.
I'm eager to oblige when asked
To judge their serious disputes.
These tiny terrors
With opinionated views.
I weigh their arguments as best I can
Because, sometimes I'm confused.
Basketballs pound, screams sound
While Footballs bang walls.
Drowning parents repeated calls.
Some prefer a Soccer ball.
Bicycles, Scooters, and Skateboards
In daredevil speed
Often run into you
For no apparent need.
As their sad little faces
Try to apologize
And debate you when you tell them
That it is just not wise.
Still some folks wish they'd vanish
In trade for peace and quiet.
But they've got a right to play
Being rookies.
To expect my yes
To their usual quest.
"Amigo You Got Cookies."

Are You Pessimist or Optimist?

The Pessimist:
A house is worth a thousands words
Beginning with Rent
And ending with Eviction

The Optimist:
A house is worth a thousand words
Beginning with Buy
And ending with Sell

The Pessimist:
The longer you live the longer you die
The Optimist:
The longer you live the more you survive

The Pessimist:
There isn't a day I don't feel
What is worth to do

The Optimist:
There isn't a day I don't feel
A dream is coming true

The Pessimist (constant distraction)
The Optimist (positive action)

Bushmen (a-z challenge)

Active Bushmen Congregate
Debate
Eatable Flesh Grazing Heartily
Inadvertently Juxtapose
Kookaburra's Laughter
Manifest Nearby Ominous Peril
Quietly Reaching Stalking Targets
Unite Vulnerable Warning
Xing Yields Zapping

Chances Are You Will

Laugh, take a bath, sing, buy a ring
Hum, appear dumb, pry, begin to cry
Walk, talk, balk, run, have fun
Skip, take a trip, jump, stomp
Love, snub, get shoved, have a back rub
Date, be late, wait, hate
Drive, stride, ride, slide
Beg, break a leg, rave, shave
Pray, sway, delay, weigh
Be nice, entice, sacrifice
Dance, prance, chance, romance
Lie, deny, signify
Take, forsake, steal, appeal
Give, relive, ponder, wonder
Be stressful, successful
And boast to hide your weakness
At lease once a day
But only if you're human.

Did I Give In, Or Give Up?
(pantoum)

Did I give in, or give up?
On the day we finally parted
The consent was too abrupt
To feel broken hearted

On the day we finally parted
Was I agreeing to be free?
To feel broken hearted
Was this really truly me?

Was I agreeing to be free?
Accepting solitary
Was this really truly me?
And was it necessary?

Accepting solitary
I would finally be alone
And was it necessary
To release the love I've known?

I would finally be alone
The consent was too abrupt
To release the love I've known
Did I give in, or give up?

Dispute Between Two Gods

Ode to Mythology

Boldly denying Her promised visits
Rain has angered Sun
And ignited His wrath with teasing clouds
That refuse to yield Her waters of vitality

Enraged Sun sends forth infernal heat
And scourges the land of life
Destroying trees, plants, grasslands,
And all within His fiery path

Burning homes to obliteration
Claiming litters of panic-stricken animals
Sacrificing all humans unable to survive
Sun's merciless unbearable heat

Although He's been accused of it
Wind does not take sides
When fueling these flames of anger
He just blows his course

Who should we blame, Rain or Sun?
Neither
Be humble when gods quarrel
Once one forgives the other
They will replenish the fruits of life.

Don't You Tell Nobody

Forbidden Secrets

Don't you tell nobody where you've been
If the road you travel dips in sin
They're going to claim temptation
Has tainted your salvation
Even if you swear you didn't give in
There is just one way to save your skin
Don't you tell nobody what you've seen
If what you saw deserves the guillotine
No matter how you tell it
They'll twist it and they'll sell it
Knowing they can place you at the scene
They will try to force you to come clean
Traveling down life's road facing episodes
Some things are better left untold
Don't you tell nobody what you do
If the truth is going to punish you
Because deceitful ears
Tell everything they hear
Especially if the subject is taboo
They can't hardly wait to rat on you

Giving Is Always Something Nothing Always Needs

Giving is always something
Nothing always needs
When you practice true the former
The latter always feeds

How foolish it is to censure
The will to succeed
When idle is free to venture
Through this bestowing deed

Nothing needs transition
Give your soul ambition
Educate yourself forever
It's beneficial to be clever

Some goals may be polluted
It still is unrefuted
If aims were meant to fail
Not one dream would prevail

Dreams Will Awaken (senryu)

To all goal tenders

In a distant time
If plans stay true to purpose
Dreams will awaken

Gullable Ears (senryu)

Swear not what you hear
Seek out the final judgement
Truth hides in research.

Zowie (senryu)

Zig-zagging zebra
Zooming, zestfully zowie
Zip zonked zookeeper

Vintner (senryu)

To Rd3feathers

Vig, Vintage Vintner
Violently Vinified
Vinegared Vines Vim

God's Desire For Universal Peace

He guides my pen, I pray.

The World has one huge problem
It spills it's blood to shun
God's Desire For Universal Peace
To each and everyone

Those who think their religion
Is the only one He hears
Support the wrong decision
And pollute our atmospheres

His universal guidelines
Has taught us to survive
All who seek His laws for peace
Even our spiritual tribes

His rainforests hold the secrets
To all our earthly needs
Destroy them and you kill all life
Depending on their seeds

By discovering alien life
We may benefit each other
But let's secure our world
Before we seek another.

Gossip

When you allow gossip to
Cloud your thoughts with resentment
Pump your heart with anger
Whisper into trusting ears
And soothe them with discomfort

Disturb and thrash a pleasant mood
Dominate an interlude
Reveal secrets that should have been kept
Awaken cruel schemes that should have slept
Bring tears to a happy face
Shame, sorrow, and disgrace

Mingle in the highest court of law
And adjudicate it's reachings
Settle in the holy gatherings
And demonize their teachings

Leave true friends with doubts of authenticity
Destroy peace and promote misery
Make hearsay common grounds for divorce
Be a dream's main driving force

Disaffirm honest donations
Falsify appreciations
Don't blame all these heartless ruinations
On inquiring mind's anticipation.

Grandma's Oscar Performance

My grandchildren are coming today
They'll certainly want to toy me
This is no time for peace of mind
I hope they will enjoy me

I'll embrace their laughter
When riotous games unfold
And cherish their happy faces
More precious than pure gold

I'll give them extra cookies
Each time they opt to please me
And hide behind a frown
How it tickles when they tease me

So they won't see my sadness
When it's time to depart
I'll pretend I'm filled with gladness
To hide my aching heart

Great Grand Niece, London Is In Heaven

To Sharon with love, Uncle Alvin

Twelve forevermore, an irreplaceable glow
Taken by the angels I keep telling myself.
Instantly crushed, never knowing how much
She meant in my fond memories.
Fate has frozen her lovingness in my mind
At a stop light in the traffic of life
Some repeated offender over ran
And killed her mother Stacey also.

When I lived above them in her grandfather,
My late brother's house she would climb the
Stairs and knock, "Uncle Alvin, it's London."
"What do you want?" I'd teasingly reply.
Her smile lit up my whole day.
I'm far away from that fatal scene.
That claimed this child of so much promise.
I won't make the funeral, so eulogistically
I'll enshrine her memorial here
Forevermore, along with my condolences.
May both mother and daughter rest in peace.

Homeless In New York With Pride

Those who are

Hard times the offing, New York was scoffing
With jobs no one desired
Dishwashers were needed, the work was depleted
You always could get hired

If I didn't detour, I knew for sure
One day I'd have my own place
So on pay day I'd stash away
At Manhattan's bank called Chase

First pay I stopped at a thrift shop
And brought a suit for show
If a homeless man could proudly stand
No one would ever know

The Roosevelt, I always felt
Had free accommodations
The usual test, get pass the desk
Before the realizations

My entrance was grand, a newspaper and
A briefcase always empty
A confident smile would always beguile
Those expecting tips a plenty

In the rear, a staircase so dear
Seldom used for climbing
Was where I'd rest at a maid's request
It all took perfect timing

You had to be bold, when nights were cold
Sleeping on the subway trains
A truck load of cops would board the last stop
And take to jail your remains

But in my suit, one couldn't refute
A business man quite tired
Who's toiled away a heavy day
Someone to be admired

A gentle nudge, my eyes would judge
A conductor or a cop
Wake up I'm sure it's after four
Sir, you've overslept your stop

Years would pass before at last
Those restless days would end
Sweat and grime, The New York Times
Would become my best friend.

How Can Love Survive
If We're Not Willing

What's it like trying to live without you?
What's a melody without a tune?
How can a day be happy with no sunshine?
How can a night be perfect with no moon?

How can love survive if we're not willing
To forgive the fury of a storm?
And when the chill of anger is within us,
How can empty arms keep us warm?

If there's no room for compassion
How can we share the same dream?
I don't know your true intentions.
I just know how much it would mean.

If only you would stay with me forever.
Willing to face all the ups and downs.
I would give my heart and soul to you completely,
In a love that's truly heaven-bound.

How Can You Bribe A Nation?

How can you bribe a nation
When the contract isn't fair
And so many eyes can see
The promises aren't there?

You force with so much power
A will that won't atone
Disregarding tyranny lessons
Of great nations over-thrown

And you justify your wars
Where freedom lacks in reason
And greed's the only substance
Fueling acts of treason

And compensating lost ones
With more atrocities
How can you bribe a nation
With no democracies?

I Ain't Doing Nothing Without The Lord

The cotton pickers

You can work my bones from dawn to dusk
And I don't care how long you fuss
I ain't doing nothing without the Lord
'Cause the treasures in His pay check
You can not afford

You won't keep me down 'cause I believe
He will make sure that I succeed
I ain't doing nothing without the Lord
'Cause the treasures in His pay check
You can not afford

You can shout out directions
Like you got me on a string
Jesus is my protection
So your bark don't mean a thing

You can pave the road with no advances
I'll walk with Him and take my chances
I ain't doing nothing without the Lord
'Cause the treasures in His pay check
You can not afford.

I Want To See It Happen

Be patient with your dreams

What good is praise to an artist
If time runs out before the glory?
Only God can see the farthest
How will the sun shine in my story?

Enthusiastically I tremble
As thoughts invade the issue
If the craftsman's deeds escape the limbo
Just how much will they miss you?

It seems it doesn't matter
If I'm not around to witness
The praise and all the chatter
Never seeing proof of fitness

Epitaphs are simply stated
Of true masters, here lies one
Still I dread it if I'm slated
After death to be renown

So don't promise supposition
For my efforts to ascend
If I'm due some recognition
I want to see it happen.

I Will

To Jesus (God)

If You say go forth, I will
And seek out, I will
All the lonely lost souls
That my arms can hold
I will

If You say break bread, I will
Until all is fed, I will
Knock on every door
Until hunger is no more
I will

Lord I'll do your bidding
And I won't waste time sitting
Around while others pain
You just point the way
And I'll spend every day
Busy helping someone in Your Name

If You say stand strong, I will
And fight wrong, I will
Because I'm in Your Army
Ain't nothing can harm me, I will

And no matter what they're shoving
Just keep right on loving
I will

Ideas Playing Horseshoes

Ideas competing for iron-clad substance
Hurl repeatedly back and forth
Like playing a game of Horseshoes
Slamming against the pillars of acceptance
Each one vying to be a ringer

Facing off to prove their worth
Spinning around the poles of probability
Well aimed Ideas cling secured
Those too weak to grasp sufficiency
Are rejected and labeled useless

Some Ideas launch humiliation
Chasing disaster plagued by laughter
Like Horseshoes running amuck
Uprooting status and mowing shame
In their efforts to escape the fiasco

When all exertions are weighed and filed
Each event of unused concepts
Is replayed to the clangor of failure
Where all rejected ideas echo
Like the agony of losing the game

If I Didn't Have You

I'd feel so much pain
In these eyes of mine
There'd be constant rain
Pleasures turned around
Goodtimes upside down
In love would be a thrill I never knew
If I didn't have you
All this would be true

If I didn't have you
Storms would find a way
Into my happy heart
And wreck each sunny day
Joy would come to past
Misery would outlast
Any and all efforts to subdue
The lonely years I suffered and withdrew
If I didn't have you
Birds would seize to sing
Life wouldn't mean a thing

If It Takes Forever

To God

If it takes forever
I will learn to fly
With only good intentions
And I will soar so high
He'll reach out and touch me
And Shower me with Grace
In his mighty kingdom
I will earn a space
If it takes forever

I believe He truly is forgiving
And loving Him has made my life worth living

If it takes forever
I will spend the time
Fleeing from temptation
Seeking peace of mind
Above the storms of hatred
Jealousy and pain
Someday up in Heaven
My soul will remain

Taco (sedoka)

Tiny Terror

Taco is a dog
Tiny and ferocious beast
If you disturb his night walks

He will show his teeth
Followed by a vicious growl
Large dogs have respect for him

More About Taco

He's Jack Russell and Chihuahua
With quite a mean bow-wow
When these two mixed tempers show their force
If he takes you by surprise
And you don't see his size
He can even spook a policeman's horse

He has a group of walkers
Which he protects from stalkers
They don't miss a turn to hold his lease
When he is on patrol
The underworld knows
They ain't got a chance to break the peace

And yet, this fender-bender
Can really be quite tender
If you're one of the lucky few he likes
And of those few he picks
He showers them with licks
And he'll insist that they enjoy his hikes

He's a Hollywood star
Hail, this tiny czar
Shunning all the eager shouts and waves
When he prances by
Fans eat humble pie
They don't mind the way that he behaves

My Cousin Elmer Hill

To Barbera and Pam with Love

Kind, gentle, and understanding
Was my cousin Elmer Hill
His quiet wisdom was never demanding
To advise you was his will
His philanthropic heart
Was always giving
He made your life
Seem more worth living
He never complained of any pain
Through the wonderful times we shared
He found relief in how you felt
This man really cared
When you speak of great ones
And shoes to fulfill
There was no nicer person then
My Cousin Elmer Hill

Never Better (rondolet)

To Mbrdidely (Bob) and Karen M. Miner

Never Better
Living in a time of plenty
Never Better
Able to endeavor whether
To save ten or to spend twenty
Feeling dolce far niente
Never Better

Often (rictameter)

Helping those in need

Often
My deepest thoughts
Launch an urge inside me
Not to give in to those in need
Helping folks can sometimes be so draining
But because I am able to
Help their situations
I endure them
Often

One Whole Day
And What Goes In It

Amorous affections from pleasant dreams
Or nightmares with ridiculous schemes
In full swing and on a roll
Or all dressed up and no place to go
A scintillating gregarious flower
Or a pessimistic seizure hour after hour
A perceived orator with precise intent
Or trying to explain just what you meant
Keeping up with a winning pace
Or running full speed in the wrong race
Money plus your biggest problem
Or credit cards and how to solve them
You made your point and it was good
Or totally misunderstood
You knew exactly what you were doing
Or it's your fault your day was in ruin
You trade your dreams to lie awake
Or you can't sleep for your mistakes
Good or bad we're forced to spend it
One whole day and what goes in it.

Our People's Needs

Fix America's problems first!

How long must we suffer?
And who cares what we think?
What'll we do with all this water
That isn't fit to drink?

The sun no longer warms
These over-soaken bones
How many have lost their lives?
The count is still unknown

Once this striving city
Sheltered so much life
We'll need more than pity
To mend it's sacrifice

Will this nation learn it's lesson?
To grow stronger we must share
And spend our money wisely
On Our People's Needs, then elsewhere

Poet Ashantewarrior
(Organizer of Your Thoughts)

His words will fill your soul with reasons
When your heart is set on romance
He'll fire your yearns throughout the seasons
When your feelings must have substance

You think of hate and he'll inject
Sound reasons of forgiving
His words of wisdom will project
Much better ways for living

His subjects cover every phase
Of trials and tribulations
Just read them and you'll be amazed
With his sincere dedications

So when your thoughts have cause to roam
And you can't find solutions
Ashantewarrior is always home
Just read his resolutions

Poet Danny Elliott
(Patron of God's Love)

He's easy to approach
And oh so understanding
God's given him a broach
A metal for withstanding

Temptations that have altered
The life's of those who hate
His pen has never faltered
To praise his love and faith

And when you read his findings
You'll see a great contender
Who's heart's set on reminding
The wealth of God's defenders

Poetess Karen M. Miner
(Conqueror of Poetic Forms)

She specializes in existing
Poems of vast exciting styles
Once you plunge there's no resisting
Volumes of her fabulous files

She'll dazzle you with her renditions
Of Pantoums with repeated lines
Romance her Trois-Par-Huit admission
With candlelights where lovers dine

Her Ottava-Rima went number one
Her efforts were outstanding
Dodge the devil with her Nonet run
Her Rondels are commanding

There's Etherees and Villanelles
Abcedarians
Limericks and Kyrielles
She'll teach you every trend

Excuse me while I stall............
No room to name them all!

Poetess Arkay Evans
(The Conscience of Your Soul)

Her forceful words may seem abusive
To those who have reason to hide
Behind spoiled curtains most conducive
To years of practice genocide

Wars and greed have no foundation
Avarice souls exposed and haunted
Peace will win her confirmation
When equal shares survive the gauntlet

Ah, but when she loves she truly shares
All the passion of a giving heart
If you seek wisdom from one who dares
Arkay will rip your doubts apart.

Poetess Jay5, Queen of Limericks

Miss poet who's name is Jay5
Is bursting our guts with her jive
Her Limericks are funny
Make gloomy days sunny
Rib-tickling, sidesplitting archives

Poetess Gungalo
(Chief Judge of Poetry)

She voice's truth, there's no pretext
With prose worth ascertaining
She's to the point, never complex
And thoroughly entertaining

She'll tell you what you need to know
And if you're thinking clear
Her words will cause an overflow
Of gratitude and cheer

She's world reknown and serves us well
When poems need reviewing
The value of their worth she'll tell
With no misconstruing

Humor is her greatest gift
Laughter roars like thunder
When you want the perfect lift
Seek this living wonder!

Poetess Living Sacrifice
(so young, so wise, so gifted.)

It's amazing how someone so young
Can be so knowledgeable in prose
The wisdom it takes one years to tongue
Living Sacrifice already knows

Her work is so astounding
The praises have begun
To hear voices resounding
This living phenomenon

So let's not crowd this budding flower
I don't mean to petition
And someday she will proudly tower
In full earned recognition

Quaint Quaker's Quality

Quaint Quaker's Quality
Quantified Quantum Quotes
Quietly Quashing Queen's
Questionable Quasi Queasy Quarrel
Quaker's Quixotic Quittance Quest
Quitclaimed Queen's Quowarranto
Quipping Questionable Quorum
Qualifying Quaker's Quietus
Quarrantining Queen's Qualm

Love May Return

Today I suffer
I miss the love she gave me
Yesterday we shared
Now only memories live
Tomorrow love may return

Wanderer (w-challenge)

To Hydrine's challenge

Wishful wanderer's wary wane
Wanting wonderous wizardly wonders

Woven wrought wryly welcome
Wyverns wrath, with writhen worshiping's
Worthlessly wonted woe

Witnessed wizards wittingly whirl
Worthily worshipped wands

Wrath whipping wanderer's
Whimsical whereinto
Whatever witchery wacked-out
Wade well-wisher waffled

Wag wanderer's wail-ful
Warp wagers wrestling
Wasted warlock wangling

Wonders, where waits, when
Welcome warranties

Rediscovering Holiday Devotion

Holding fast to amorous passion
I'll tug the lease of yearning
And hope on Happy Valentine's Day
The wheels of love are turning

Giving gifts at Christmas Time
I try to be the first one
On New Year's Eve I set a goal
To be a better person

Thanksgiving Day I quote His wisdom
Blessing food with prayer
Rediscovering Jesus' promise
Easter has a special flair

On Veterans Day I'll march with pride
To honor the price our heroes paid
And with each step resound old glory
At The Independence Day Parade

For my Mother and Father
Who's devotion has paved the way
I will rediscover a flower
On their special Holidays

Rhyme

No doubt there's far less freedom
From inception to conclusion
Words must fit where you need them
With no room for illusion

The beauty of their dance
Would make a poet blush
Should one dare to chance
The tango of their thrust

A poem can be tragic
And quite operatic
To think rhyme lacks it's magic
Is simply pathetic

And you can even sing
The thoughts of your creation
In harmony with zing
When rhyme is your foundation

When all is said and done
The journey most to please one
Will certainly be more fun
To rhyme your way through reason.

She Believed She Was A Rose (part 1)

The times, they were so hard
Conditions made no sense
Still this homeless little child
Somehow wasn't quite convinced
Piercing through the misery
She could plainly see
Herself among the flowers
Free of poverty
In torn and tattered clothes
She Believed She Was A Rose
Her daddy die in shame
To weak to overcome
The sadness in his heart
For the things he hadn't done
Mother couldn't get over it
Drugs replaced romance
The child barring the burden
Still found time to dance
Balanced on her toes
She Believed She Was A Rose

She Believed She Was A Rose (part 2)

Cindy Lee believed she was a rose
Even in her torn and tattered clothes

Now fighting poverty
Passing laws for those in need
Congresswoman Cindy Lee
Is among the hero breed
This woman full of passion
Is that same little girl
Who never stop believing
Now speaking to the world
As destiny unfolds
In torn and tattered clothes
She always knew she was a Rose

Cindy Lee believed she was a rose
Even in her torn and tattered clothes.

So Lonely And So Blind

To all the unloved Children

So lonely is the child
Who's thoughts are forbidden
So blind the enforcer
Who's ignorance is hidden
Their paths through life
Are fruitlessly stridden
Where dreams are restricted
And failures are bidden
Creative desires
Restrained and chidden
Eventually succumb to midden
Two life's face disaster
Hate becomes their master
Visualize the sadness
Misanthropic madness
An impasse worth good ridden.

Tainted Pride (nonet)

Through word of mouth I stumbled into
some unkind slurs of one provoked.
Who cursed a pastor's sermon
for lack of funds to give
to the churhes needs.
When asked to leave
tears replaced
tainted
pride.

Stew-Pendous.Com

Stew-Pendous.Com
Is where I rest my case
All this creative talent
I can't afford to waste

I've written a few books
And songs of which are plenty
And drew a few cartoons
Because Leftover's was empty

Stand up comedy
Is where I'll venture next
My debut is on video
And laughter fills the text

If you're a smart investor
With an eye for what can sell
Once we share each other's needs
I'm sure we'll earn quite well

Yes, I've got a web site
For the whole world to eye
So if you find the time
Take a peek and you'll see why?

The Children of Our Nation

To a child's right to love

Children have so much love
For their new found friends
With no hatred forced between
Their different colored skins

Until that love is altered
By some misguided peers
Who's bias education
Ruins their joyful cheers

No laws protect the children
Who's minds we simply steal
One day in retribution
They'll play the cards we deal

And death will come with anger
That never had a chance
To befriend a stranger
And avoid the circumstance

When will we ever learn
To stand for segregation
Will poison and destroy
The Children of Our Nation

The Wealth Of God's Defenders

They dwell among the rich
And live among the poor
In circumstances which
They're blessed forevermore

The power of their faith
God's laws of absolution
With no platforms for hate
Or practiced destitution

They care about each other
All bare their burden share
Freeing sister and brother
From the clutches of despair

They never have the problems
Of those obsess with greed
Their will to share dissolves them
Their minds are trouble freed

Valued assets tally wrong
You're only rich pretenders
Until you place your funds among
The Wealth Of God's Defenders

They All Are Worth The Prize

Children see us laugh and children see us cry
Children see us live and children see us die
Still they return the smile of each passer by
If you honestly enjoy them it's you they
Satisfy. Isn't this sound reason to more than
Wonder why some folks want to change the love
Within their eyes? With segregated feelings
Base on selfish enterprise to conceal the
Truth
They All Are Worth The Prize
Oh children of today wake up and realize
If it brings so much sorrow how can hate be
Justified? Wallow in your goodness and share
Your precious toys, play long with your true
Friends and one day winds of joy will blow
Away this evil and profoundly rectify
When it comes to Children
They All Are Worth The Prize
"Love Personified"

Treachery

Trapped
In the web of treachery
Tangled in deceit
A trusting heart no more.

T-Ball (tanka)

T-Ball is a sport
Tiny tots play eagerly
Until they tire
Their parents can't wait to see
Them in Baseball's Hall Of Fame

God (haiku)

All we'll ever need
Is within His planted seed
God sows life take heed

Un Relinquish Love

Night's upon us, love has drawn us
Here where it truly wants us
In each other's arms before the dawn

Please invite me, hold me tightly
Caress this flame inside me
Let's make love before the night is gone

Whatever will be gives no warning
But I've wanted you for so long
What will I do in the morning
If you should decide this was wrong

Want to please me, say you need me
That you will never leave me
Even in the fury of a storm

Chance's you may see it my way
Come dawn and share a new day
Un Relinquish Love to keep us warm

We Must Accept Each Other

I promise to shun never
This task I must endeavor
Inform my fellow poet
And those who don't yet know it

That I'm a giving person
Who seldom needs coercion
To rise to the occasion
Or reasons for evasion

When someone writes a challenge
To accept and not infringe
Upon their right to create
A puzzle worth a debate

To support one another
We must accept each other

Wedlock Thoroughbred

Wedlock Thoroughbred
Love is not his choice to make
Only bred for speed

He is forced to run
Track records show a winner
Often he will lose

Selective breeding
The day he's sent to pasture
Still not free to choose

Which Way Was I Going? (pantoum)

Confussion

Which way was I going
When the sun refused to shine?
The wear and tear was showing
From the dreams I left behind

When the sun refused to shine
Was I simply out of touch
From the dreams I left behind
I had come to love so much?

Was I simply out of touch
With my destiny's chosen path?
I had come to love so much
Was I doing all my math?

With my destiny's chosen path
As I pondered indecision
Was I doing all my math?
Was I simply in transition?

As I pondered indecision
The wear and tear was showing
Was I simply in transition?
Which way was I going?

Who Can You Trust For Sure?

The one who wakes you anxiously
To see you through your day
And whatever sport you crave
Is ever so eager to play

They won't shed a single tear
When you pour out your troubles
But every single word they'll hear
As long as you blow bubbles

When you need some company
They'll snuggle in your arms
And when danger can't be seen
They'll sound the first alarm

If you haven't guessed by now
Who fills your life with hope
You never would have anyhow
It's your dog, slow poke

Non-animal lovers
Need not be offended
And for those who can't afford a pet
No harm was intended.

Who Is Really In Control

When you rest your thoughts
Your mind never sleeps
It's always creating adventures
Some, nightmares, dark and deep
Those who work on little sleep
Abusing it's existence
Should get their proper rest
And not cater to resistance
In dreams it often warns us
of what could be detrimental
Our unpredictable mind
Can be sometimes sentimental
Many a fender-benders
Consider themselves blessed
Being jolted out of day dreams
While their mind was on a quest
There are millions of situations
Your mind must explore
Honor it's trek. When tired, rest!
And respect it's endless chore.

Why blame Color?

To those who can't see beyond color.

When someone wants a better deal
With no just reason to repeal
Why blame Color?

There's no sane cause for genocide
If greed is what you're trying to hide
Why blame Color?

If someone dear decides to roam
And chose a darker honeycomb
Why blame Color?

If love's a fear to contemplate
Because you're sick inside with hate
Why blame Color?

If the blood you need to stay alive
Is gathered from a different tribe
Why blame Color?

While working your dreams to succeed
If you can't find the peace you need
Why blame Color?

When underneath it's hue
Brave hearts are pumping love.

Wishful's Sleepless Dreams (Pentaphor)

Hopeful Events

Huge Expectations
Force only cat naps
Worked aggravations
Fear total collapse
Dodging the mind traps

Intrusively
Insanity
Indulgently
Insist to be

Nagging thrust
Thoughts can't trust
Sending us

Into
Undo

Hope.

The Prophet

Standing at the gates of hell
On a platform billed for dying
Evildoer he befell
Telling truths, accused of lying

Many saddening faces mournful
Of the facts he wouldn't deny
And his executioners scornful
Of his justified reply

You who will not share your wealth
Are basking in confusion
Detrimental to your health
With purified illusions

You who feel so safe within
The confines of your greed
Will perish from the guilt within
The curse of your misdeeds

For on this day I say to you
I'm standing where I should be
If no one here can see into
How rich a giver could be

Punishment won't fit the crime
If death is your decision
Years of ponder will in time
Kill dreams of acquisition

What good does it to win a war
If peace is still illusive
And losers are forever sore
And winners still abusive?

The hangman cried and yelled "I can't."
This seer deserves to live
Before I fill this awful grant
My own life I will give

The crowd began to back his claim
"Free the humble sage."
And when they did, they only blamed
The angry throng's rage

www.ingramcontent.com/pod-product-compliance
Lightning Source LLC
Chambersburg PA
CBHW032217040426
42449CB00005B/634